COME ON A JOURNEE WITH ME TO NYC

CREATED BY FRED WHITAKER
WRITTEN BY COURTNEY WHITAKER
ILLUSTRATED BY CAMERON WILSON

To Journee and Briley: You two young women are my daily motivation and inspiration. The world is yours.

To my fellow Black fathers: "We are vital to our children's preparation beyond educational curricula not written by us." Lead by example. Share our stories. Support one another. Learn from one another.

Fred Whitaker Jr

Today is the big day! Journee, her cousin Briley, and her pet dog Oreo are finally going on an adventure with her dad.

Journee and Briley have been dreaming about this day all week. They couldn't wait to see the Big Apple.

Journee asked, "Daddy can we see Central Park while you're at work?"

"Of course you can babygirl." He agreed while packing up the car. Briley squealed as she replied, "I've been studying maps all week."

"Whoa! Look at the tall buildings." uttered Journee.

"This is the biggest and coolest city I've ever seen." Briley declared.

"Okay girls, while I'm at work. You three can explore the city. Be Careful." Encouraged Fred.

"We will Daddy. We love you" the girls replied. As Oreo ruffed goodbye.

With a map in their hands, the girls headed to the train station. "It's time to finally see Central Park!" Journee loudly chimed.

The train was filled to the brim with street performers.
"Look at those dancers! The singers!" Briley proclaimed.

"I want to learn how to do that Briley! Let's practice
when we get home." Journee decided.

HARLEM

Amazed by the performances, they accidentally missed their stop.
"Uh oh!" cried Briley. "I think we missed our stop."

As they exited the train station, the beautiful colorful city of Harlem appeared.

"Wow, this place is awesome!" Journee marveled.

While Journee was excited, Briley was worried about how they would get to Central Park.

"The map says all we have to do is walk two blocks, make a left and we can get back on a new train.

Let's go!" pointed out Briley.
"Okay, and maybe we can explore Harlem along the way," Journee added.

As the girls started to walk towards the train station, they came across a museum, packed with stunning pictures of Black history.

"Oh my Briley. Look at this place."
Journee whispered in awe."Look at all the art. I've never seen people who look like us painted like this before." squealed Briley.

Out of nowhere, as they left the museum. Oreo suddenly took off. "Oh no, Oreo!" screamed Briley. Journee and Briley chased behind Oreo in the opposite direction of the train!

Oreo ran into the Atomic Wing's Restaurant.

Journee, Briley, and Oreo ate the delicious food Chef Cynthia gave them.

"Now that you three have full bellies for the rest of your adventure, is there anything else, you need help with?"Cynthia asked."Yes please, can you tell us how to get to Central Park?" Journee replied.

"Of course, all you have to do is walk outside and make a left." said Cynthia.

APOLLO

WELCOME TO HARLEM'S WORLD FAMOUS APOLLO THEATER

As the girls walked to the train station, they came across the world famous Apollo theater!"

Doesn't Uncle Fred have a meeting here Journee?" questioned Briley.

"Yes, he does!" exclaimed Journee.

When they entered the theater,
they found Fred hard at work.

"Daddy! We tried to find Central Park, but we got lost." Journee admitted. Briley excitedly shared, "Instead, we found a museum, a wing spot restaurant and got to see Harlem."

"It sounds like you two had a big day. Let's go home." said Fred.

The girls were sad as they took a taxi cab back to the hotel.
"Man, I really wanted to see Central Park." Briley huffed to herself.

"Me too, but we did get to go on an epic adventure instead."
Journee mentioned.

Briley agreed.

"Okay girls, let's get ready for bed." uttered Fred, as he opened the hotel room blinds.

"OMG! Journee look!" gasped Briley.
Behind the blinds, stood Central Park in all its glory.

"It was underneath us all along, all we had to do was look!" Journee cheered.

THE
END

Made in the USA
Columbia, SC
10 November 2020

Journee ENTERPRISES

CAM DA ILLA STRATA

9 781735 621715

$12.99

ISBN 978-1-7356217-1-5

51299>

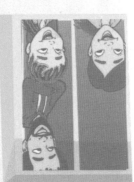

COME ON A JOURNEE WITH ME to NYC

When Journee and Briley Miles join their father for his work trip to New York City. The young girls accidentally stumble upon an epic adventure. Together, with the help of their dog Oreo, they discover the hidden gems and culture of the city.